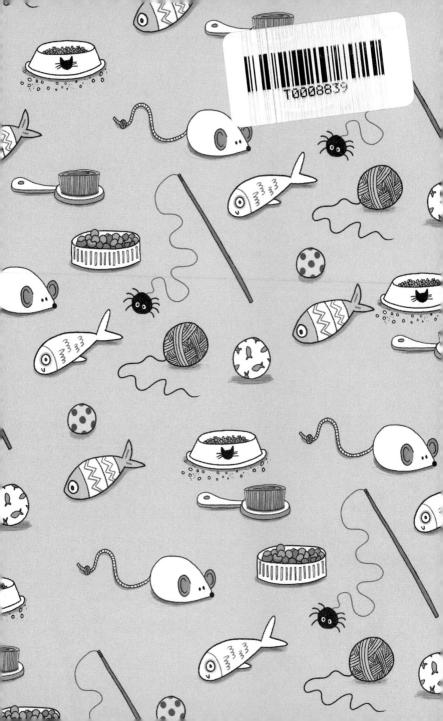

A FIRST GUIDE TO

CATS

UNDERSTANDING YOUR WHISKERED FRIEND

by Dr. John Bradshaw
illustrated by Clare Elsom

Penguin Workshop

PENGUIN WORKSHOP
An imprint of Penguin Random House LLC, New York

First published in Great Britain by Andersen Press Limited, 2022

First published in the United States of America by Penguin Workshop,
an imprint of Penguin Random House LLC, New York, 2023

Text copyright © 2022 by John Bradshaw
Illustrations copyright © 2022 by Clare Elsom

Photo credits: cover: (lines) Dimitris66/DigitalVision Vectors/Getty Images;
(ribbon) Fourleaflover/iStock/Getty Images

Visit us online at penguinrandomhouse.com.

Library of Congress Cataloging-in-Publication Data is available.

Manufactured in Canada

ISBN 9780593521854   10 9 8 7 6 5 4 3 2 FRI

Dedicated to all cats everywhere,
but especially for Pippin, Fotheringay,
Splodge, Lucy, Frisky, and
the real Libby—JB

For Ted & Elvis,
and their fantastic humans,
Candice, Matt, and Lochy—CE

Hello!

I'm Dr. John Bradshaw.

I'm a biologist, but unlike the biologists
who study wild animals, I have spent a lot of
time studying people's pets. I find cats especially
fascinating because their lives are quite private,
even though they're happy to share their homes
with us. This book will help you to know
what the world would be like if you were
a cat. We're going to follow a day in the
life of Libby, a cat I know well, and
the people she lives with.

Libby

It's five o'clock on an autumn morning in an ordinary street on the outskirts of town. Still dark. The milkman's van glides around the corner, and its headlights briefly reveal two green eyes on the top of a garden wall. A shadowy shape trots across the road and then away, between the houses.

Meet **Libby**. She's a four-year-old black-and-white cat, and she's checking out the neighborhood before it gets too busy. Libby is quite an anxious cat, and doesn't like surprises, so the hour before dawn is one of her favorite times to go outdoors. She's used to the milkman, though, and isn't bothered that her shining eyes might have given her away.

Why did Libby's eyes glow in the light? Yours don't! It's because cats' eyes need to gather as much light as possible, so they can see where they're going at night. When you look at something, a lot of the light that gets into your eyes doesn't get picked up by your brain, and just disappears into your skull. Cats —and foxes, and lots of other animals that go out at night—have a sort of mirror at the back of their eyes (called a "tapetum") that gives their brain a second chance to catch the light. After the light has been reflected, some of it escapes back out through the front of their eyes. Creepy? Not if you're a cat, just part of everyday life—or rather, every-night life.

Cats' eyes are special in other ways, too, allowing them to see much better than us when it's dark. They're huge compared to the size of their heads, almost as big as ours. And their pupils (that's the black circle in the middle) can get even bigger than ours do, especially at night, so they can let lots of light in.

Libby is round the back of the houses now, crisscrossing from one garden wall to the next on her way home. She remembers that sometimes there's a dog in one of the gardens, so before she jumps off the wall, she listens carefully to check whether he's been let out yet. Without moving her head, she turns each ear to the side, one to the left, the other to the right. Cats' standing-up ears can be pointed in almost any direction, so they can find out where a sound is coming from and how far away it is. Our ears are quite good at doing that, but they'd hear even better if we could wiggle them one at a time (why don't you try?).

All Libby can hear now is the squeaking of a bat on its way home, tired after a night catching moths and looking forward to a

day's sleep hanging upside-down in the roof of the old church hall. Cats can hear lots of very high-pitched sounds that even children's sensitive ears can only just catch, and grown-ups can't hear at all.

There's no sign of the dog, so Libby leaps down off the wall and tiptoes across the wet grass, then squeezes through a gap in the fence on the other side and into her own garden. Or rather her owner's garden. Libby thinks several gardens are "hers." Walls and fences are no barrier for a cat, just interesting places to explore or hide behind.

Cats' Coats of Many Colors

mostly black with
a few white patches

white with a
few black patches

all black cat

Libby has a black-and-white coat: mostly black but with a few white patches. Her white socks come from her mother, who looked just like her. A few cats are the other way around, mainly white with a few black patches, which means that both their mum and their dad had white on them.

Any cat can have white socks, not just black ones (although black and white does look very smart). Black cats are quite common, but the most common color for pet cats, and all wild cats, is

mackerel tabby

blotched tabby

tortoiseshell

brown tabby. Wild cats, and some pet cats, have narrow stripes of dark and light brown (sometimes known as mackerel tabby), but it's more usual for pet cats to have a brown coat with patches of black, which is called blotched tabby.

Tortoiseshell cats have an orange coat with black or brown patches, and are almost always female. The orange parts often come from the dad and the brown from the mum, and instead of being mixed together to make brownish orange they appear randomly all over the cat's coat, rather like a patchwork quilt.

Lost and Found

Libby lives with a schoolteacher. Everyone at school calls her "Miss Lewis," so that's what she'll be called in this book. Miss Lewis lives with Libby and her adopted daughter, Mavis (Mae for short). Libby won't care what we call either of them—cats aren't big on names.

It was Miss Lewis who gave Libby her name. Miss Lewis had thought about getting a cat for a long time, but she always seemed to be too busy, what with teaching and grading and going on trips with her friends and one thing and another (and that was all before Mae came along). Then one day she noticed a skinny cat skulking around at the end of her garden. The next day the cat was there again, and this time she meowed at Miss Lewis. The meow sounded as if it might mean "Feed me!," and Miss Lewis was thinking of having a tin of tuna for her dinner, anyway, so she went indoors, opened the tin, and put some on a saucer.

A few minutes later she realized she would have to change her plans for dinner, because the cat had eaten the lot! Once the food was gone, the cat ran off again, but the next day she came back for more food, and the next day, and the next.

Soon, Miss Lewis and the cat became friends and started sitting in the garden together, though Miss Lewis wouldn't let her in the house, because she was worried that the cat must have a proper owner somewhere nearby. But the cat kept on coming back, so one day Miss Lewis got out her phone and took a photo of her. That night she printed lots of copies of the photo on a poster that said "Is this your cat?" and the next day she pinned them up all around the neighborhood.

But no one replied. The cat was genuinely
lost.

So Miss Lewis decided she would adopt the cat herself. A pet cat needs a name, and Miss Lewis, being an educated lady, thought that any cat of hers ought to have a proper cat name. When she looked up "cat" on the internet, the first thing she found was that around the world there are more than thirty different kinds of cat. Some are well-known, like the lion and the tiger and the leopard and the cheetah, mainly because they're big and fierce.

lion   tiger   leopard   cheetah

But there are lots of kinds of smaller cats.

Some live at the tops of mountains. Others live in swamps and swim around catching fish.

But they all live on their own, and none of them like humans much. There's only one kind of cat that lives with people, and because it was first discovered in a part of North Africa called Libya, it became known as the Libyan cat. About four thousand years ago, a few Libyan cats who lived in Egypt (the country next door) changed their ways. Instead of living alone as their grandparents had done, they worked out how to make friends with people. Gradually, over hundreds of years, these special cats turned themselves into pets. Miss Lewis liked this story so much that she decided to call her new friend Libby, after the country where her ancestors might have lived.

Back to the story. It's quite light now, and Libby decides it's time for breakfast.

In through the cat flap with a *click-clack* she goes, past her empty bowl, past a pile of schoolbooks on the floor in the hall, up the stairs and into Miss Lewis's bedroom. She leaps up onto the bed and starts purring, loud enough to wake Miss Lewis up.

Cats have two different kinds of purr. One is loud and a bit harsh to listen to. Some people think that underneath the rattle of the purr itself, they can also hear a sound like a baby crying. This is the purr that cats use when they want their owners to do something for them—and NOW, not in a few minutes! The other sort of purr is much softer and means "Stay still, I'm happy here." Kittens make this purr when they want their mums to lie quietly and let them feed, and their mums reply with the same purr to make sure the kittens relax and get plenty to

eat. And of course, pet cats purr when they want to snuggle up to their favorite humans.

Miss Lewis knows this routine only too well. She knows that if she tries to ignore Libby's urgent purring, it will soon be followed up by a couple of headbutts and then some rough licking of her face. So she gets out of bed, pulls on her dressing gown, and goes downstairs to fill Libby's bowl. She makes herself a cup of tea while Libby eats, and then goes back upstairs to wake Mae.

Mae has only lived with Miss Lewis for a couple of years. She was born in India, and she doesn't know who her biological parents were. Her earliest memory is of living on the streets of a big city, and later she lived in an orphanage with lots of other lost children.

Then one day Miss Lewis came by, looking for a little girl to come and live with her. Miss Lewis stayed in a hotel near the orphanage, and saw Mae every day, so they could get to know each other really well. A few weeks later, when all the papers had been signed, Mae and Miss Lewis caught a plane back to England. To begin with, England seemed very strange to Mae—and cold!—but in her class at school there were other girls who looked like her, whose parents had been born in India, so she didn't feel out of place for long (but she still doesn't like the English winter!). And of course Libby was there, reminding her of the cats that lived around the orphanage.

Pee and Poo (and Pouncing, Too)!

Meanwhile downstairs, Libby has finished her breakfast and needs a poo. Some cats poo outdoors, often in next door's garden, but Miss Lewis doesn't want to upset her neighbors, so as soon as she'd decided to keep Libby, she bought a litter box. Libby didn't use it at first, but Miss Lewis had read that some litters are better than others, so she tried a few different brands. It turned out that Libby didn't like the gravelly kind because her paws hurt when she walked on it.

The pads on the underside of cats' feet—their "toe beans"—are the most sensitive parts of their bodies apart from their lips and the tips of their noses. That allows them to tread delicately wherever they go, and helps them keep their footing when they're walking along the top of a fence. It also means they don't like sharp gravel.

Once Miss Lewis had found a litter that Libby liked, Libby was happy to use the box.

Because she is quite a nervous cat, she had always worried about being jumped on by a dog or another cat while she was peeing or pooing out of doors. Unfortunately one day when she was using the litter box, she was scared by an unfamiliar cat peering in through the window. That quite put her off the box, and she started peeing in a corner of the hall instead. By now Miss Lewis had done a lot of research into what cats like and don't like, so she bought another litter box and put it in a quiet corner. Now Libby sometimes uses one, sometimes the other: She seems to like having a choice of where to "go." Miss Lewis keeps an eye on both trays, and scoops out the pees and poos as soon as she sees them. Cats don't like dirty litter!

Lots of cat owners get cross with their cats if they pee or poo outside their litter box, thinking that the cat is doing it on purpose just to upset them. But Miss Lewis knew better than that. She'd read that sometimes cats get so scared that they forget where the litter box is. Getting cross with a cat that's stressed out like that is only going to make things worse.

Soon it's time for Miss Lewis and Mae to leave for school. Before they go, Mae goes to the cupboard under the sink and gets out what looks like an old soda bottle. Well, it actually is an old plastic bottle, but Miss Lewis has cut a few holes in it just big enough for a cat biscuit to get through. Mae unscrews the cap from the bottle, shakes about twenty biscuits into it, and puts it down on the kitchen floor. "Goodbye, Libby," she says, and gives her a little rub on the top of her head. Libby purrs her happy purr and looks as if she might want to follow Mae out of the front door. But only for a moment; Libby remembers that the street outside is not a safe place to be during the day, and she turns back to investigate the bottle with the biscuits inside.

Cats are hunters at heart, but nowadays we don't like cats killing innocent birds and mice. A puzzle feeder like the one that Miss Lewis has made for Libby is a good way of giving a cat all the fun of hunting but without anything having to die. Libby pounces on the bottle, and it scoots away across the kitchen floor. As it goes, a biscuit falls out of one of the holes, and Libby gobbles it up.

Then she's off again, batting the bottle around the floor just as if it was a rat she wanted to kill. Every now and again a biscuit falls out, and Libby munches each one down, until she gets bored.

The sun comes out, and Libby's ready to go outside again, out through her cat flap and into the back garden. Loads of dry leaves have fallen, and when a gust of wind catches them and blows them across the lawn, Libby gets super excited, chasing them and pouncing on them as if each one was a bird or a mouse. She kind of knows that they're not, but her eyes are telling her brain that they might be. Cats' eyes are specially tuned in to things that move.

Is that a mouse, or a fox, or a leaf, or something that looks as if it might move, but doesn't, like a garden gnome?

Tiring of chasing leaves, Libby leaps up onto the fence at the bottom of Miss Lewis's garden. Unlike dogs, who usually have to go where their owners want them to, cats are too athletic to have much respect for walls and fences. They can easily walk along the top of the narrowest fence, feeling their way along with their super sensitive paws.

Of course, having four paws to balance on helps a lot, but cats are also much more supple than we are. They can put one front paw right in front of another with ease because their shoulders are only joined together at the back. Their collarbone, the bone that connects the shoulders just below the neck, is tiny. Dogs are the same, as are most mammals that run on four legs and can go faster by swinging one shoulder in front of the other.

If a cat feels that it's losing its balance, it can swing its tail the opposite way to bring itself upright again, just like a tightrope walker does with a pole at the circus. And if that doesn't work? Cats do fall from time to time, and sometimes even damage themselves, just like you would if you fell out of a tree. Strangely enough, they are most likely to get badly hurt if they fall about six feet. Cats are so supple that a fall of about three feet isn't likely to harm them. More than six feet, and they can usually land without harm. Even if they flip upside-down as they lose their grip, they can quickly twist themselves round in midair, first their shoulders, then the hips, and so land on all four outstretched legs. Libby can remember that happening to her a couple of times, but not very clearly. It's pure instinct and over in a flash. Cats are less likely to break a leg from falling than you would be, but because their heads are the heaviest part of their bodies, they sometimes bang their chins on the ground and break their bottom jaw. That needs a trip to the vet to get fixed.

Sniffling and Snuffling

Libby knows the gardens round here like the back of her paw, and also all the places where animals live. She jumps down into next door's garden and sniffs around.

SMELL NUMBER ONE: a hedgehog poo at the foot of the fence. The hedgehog lives two gardens further on in a pile of logs, and every night trundles around through gaps in the fences, looking for worms and slugs.

SMELL NUMBER TWO: next door's dog, a terrier called Rusty, has left pee and lots of smelly footprints where he's been running around just before breakfast time.

SMELL NUMBER THREE, drifting through a gap in the fence: the posh cat from two doors down, who's only let out once a day. Libby

sniffs them all carefully before walking on. She's not bothered by any of them, because she's smelled them all before and she knows that none are bad news.

You or I would barely be able to smell anything, even if we got down on all fours with our noses close to the grass. Cats can smell all sorts of things that our feeble noses can't. Everyone knows that dogs have a super sense of smell, but cats' noses are almost as sensitive as dogs' are. Also, like dogs, cats can tell a lot about something from what it smells like, often even more than from what it looks or sounds like.

SMELL NUMBER FOUR is different: another pee-smell, but this one's from a cat, and not a cat that Libby knows. It's a strong, rather yucky smell, powerful enough that you or I would easily be able to smell it, although we might not guess that it had come from a cat. That smell is there to tell Libby that the pee comes from a grown-up male cat who has been roaming the whole neighborhood for weeks. He does have a sort-of home where he gets fed, but he only goes back there every couple of days to eat and sleep. He's a cat on a mission, a mission to scare away any other male cats who might want to challenge him as the boss of the backstreets. The powerful stink of his pee is there to show how big and strong he is.

Libby looks over her shoulder quickly to see whether he might still be in sight, but after another sniff, she can tell that the pee is a few hours old. She wants to add that smell to her mental list of "cats I should keep out of the way of," so next she does something strange, something that you or I couldn't do even if we tried. She stands stock-still with her head over the stinky pee, and . . . well, she looks as though she could be growling, but there's no sound. Her top lip is curled up, showing her top row of teeth, but it's what's going on behind those teeth that's really important. A pair of little slits have opened up just behind the teeth, and she's sucking the smell up into another kind of nose, one that we don't have.

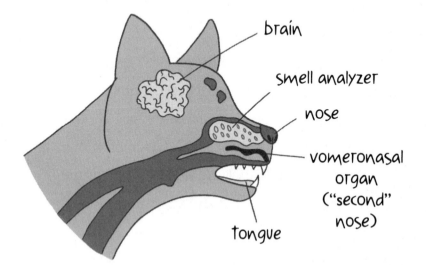

Let's call what she's doing "snuffling." Cats use this second nose (dogs have it, too) only for snuffling smells left by other cats. From this snuffling, Libby can get a better idea of how old this male cat is, how long ago he did this pee, and how often she's come across him before.

Dogs do something similar when they come across the scent of other dogs, but they don't bare their teeth at the same time, so it's harder to tell that they're doing it. If you're interested in proving to your friends that cats are smarter than dogs (or the other way around!) then here's a fun fact: Dogs' noses are more sensitive than cats'—but cats are best at snuffling.

snuffling

Libby doesn't want to draw attention to herself with such a dangerous cat about, so she wouldn't dream of having a pee anywhere nearby. Unfortunately for her, she can't help leaving a little bit of her smell behind her wherever she goes. The skin between her toes produces a little bit of scent that transfers on to everything she treads on, although it doesn't last for more than a few hours, even for a sensitive nose like a dog's or a cat's. And *our* noses can't smell anything different about the places where cats have stepped (unless they've trodden in something yucky!).

When Libby does want to leave a bit more of her scent behind, she has several ways of doing that. Cats have special glands that make a variety of scents that they can rub on to places that they want to mark. One is a little soft hairy pad under their chin; another is the skin between their eyes and their ears where there's not much hair. Another scent is made at the corners of their mouths and on their cheeks. And there's another soft pad at the end of the cat's spine, just in front of the tail. What each of these different scents means is a secret that only cats know!

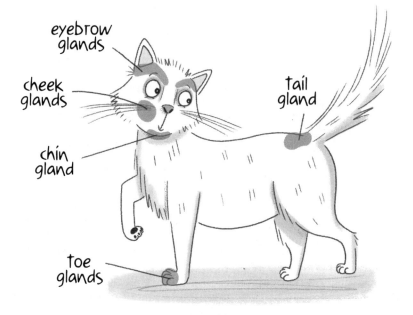

We do know that cats rub their scents off on to anything they want to mark as "theirs." This might be a fence post, or the edge of a wall, or a twig that sticks out at just the right height to catch the cat's cheek. Sometimes they will mark more than once, rubbing to and fro and then sniffing to make sure that they've left just the right amount of smell. If cats want to leave a lot of their foot-scent, they will reach up a tree trunk and drag their claws down it, leaving a scratch mark that shows where there's a scent worth sniffing!

If you see a cat rubbing on something, you can try getting down on all fours and sniffing the place, but you probably won't be able to detect anything unusual. These messages are just for other cats. They must be important, because Libby spends a lot of her time outdoors seeking out these marks and sniffing them carefully. Sometimes she will even do a little snuffle as well as just sniffing. By tracking down all the scent marks left by all the cats in the neighborhood, Libby can tell who has been out and about, and when, and also whether there are any new cats about, because every cat has a different scent, like a signature.

Friends and Neighbors

Two gardens along from her own, Libby comes across a fresh scent, one that she knows well. It belongs to her cat-friend Pippin. Maybe he's out and about, too!

Cats usually like to keep to themselves, but sometimes they can make lasting friendships with other cats. Pippin isn't a nervous cat like Libby, and he doesn't mind trying to make friends with any cat he meets. The first time Libby saw him coming, she ran back to Miss Lewis's house, bursting in through the cat flap. "Whatever's the matter?" asked Miss Lewis, but of course Libby couldn't tell her. The second time, Pippin actually came into Miss Lewis's garden, and Libby had to hide behind the summer house.

The third time, both cats happened to jump down onto the same lawn from opposite fences. This time there was no getting away without inviting a chase, so Libby froze into her "Watch out, I'm a huge cat" pose. That is, she turned sideways and all the fur on her back and her tail stood on end.

She didn't dare stare at Pippin, because to a cat that could mean "I'm going to attack you," and that was the last thing she wanted. So she looked away, while still keeping a close eye on Pippin out of the corner of her eye. Every muscle in her body was tense, even her throat, so she couldn't swallow.

After a minute or so she couldn't help saliva drooling out of the corners of her mouth.

If you'd been there, you'd probably have imagined that Libby was feeling ashamed of herself for dribbling, but cats probably can't feel ashamed—that's a human thing. She was certainly scared, though!

Pippin stopped, too. He certainly didn't want to risk getting attacked, but he did want to make friends. Cats only have one way of showing that they are feeling friendly. Dogs have lots of ways, such as wagging their tails, or bouncing up and down, or sticking their bottoms in the air and their paws out in front (called a play bow). That's because dogs have always lived in packs and so have always needed ways of talking to one another. Cats have always lived more or less by themselves and so don't have many ways of talking to one another.

But they do have one signal for "I'm your friend," and that's the one that kittens do to their mothers. They stick their tails straight up in the air before approaching. So nowadays, grown-up cats do that, too, whenever they see a cat (or a person) that they like.

Pippin's tail went up, and he kept walking slowly toward Libby. But Libby was still scared, so she took a chance and dashed away across the garden, leaped over the fence, and disappeared out of sight. Pippin, being a laid-back kind of a cat, didn't bother chasing after her, though a nasty cat might well have.

Who Can Run Faster, Libby or Usain Bolt?

When Usain Bolt runs the one-hundred-meter dash, by the time he gets halfway he's traveling at about twenty-eight miles per hour, although his average is only about twenty-three miles per hour, because it takes him a while to get up to maximum speed. Libby could probably average twenty-eight miles per hour over the first fifty meters, way ahead of Usain, but well behind what a cheetah could do (a sprinting cheetah can manage up to eighty miles per hour). However, although four legs are good for short distances, humans can outrun most other mammals over long distances. By the time Usain got to one hundred meters, he'd have caught up with Libby, and well before he'd completed his victory lap, Libby would have given up, exhausted, and hidden in the stands.

The next time their paths crossed, Libby remembered that Pippin had put his tail up, and wasn't quite so scared. Although she did run off again, it wasn't so fast. And the time after that, she very slowly raised her tail up, too, and let Pippin come up to her and sniff her face, although she still felt very tense. She remembered that a few really cunning cats may cheat, and raise their tails to pretend to be friendly, so they can get close before they pounce. But after a few more meetings had passed with no sign that Pippin might attack her, she began to relax, and tested whether Pippin was genuine by sniffing him back. And that was how their friendship began.

Today, Libby can tell that Pippin is nearby because she can smell his scent.

Over a fence she goes, and there is Pippin, sunning himself on the top of a wall. Cats love warmth. Perhaps it reminds them of the days long ago when their ancestors lived in North Africa. Those cats had very short fur so they didn't overheat, and they mainly went out at night when it was cooler. Cats that live in cold places like Norway and Canada tend to have thick fluffy fur that protects them from the snow, and some belong to special long-haired breeds such as the Norwegian Forest cat and the Maine coon (Maine isn't actually in Canada, but it's close, and just as cold!).

Pippin stands up and stretches. Up goes his tail. Up goes Libby's tail, and she runs over to him and jumps up onto the wall. They have a little sniff of each other, just to check, and then rub heads.

Greetings over, they settle down side by side,
purring away to show how happy they are to
be together. This purr is much quieter than
the purr that Libby used to wake Miss Lewis.
It's the gentle purr that cats make when they
want to be friendly, whether that's with
another cat or with a
human.

Purring is an unusual sort of noise, because it goes on continuously, whether the cat is breathing in or breathing out. Like you or me, cats can only "talk" (meow) when they've taken a breath. When cats want to meow, they tighten their vocal cords and make them vibrate, rather like a guitar string. That's the same as the way we talk. The sound of purring is made by flaps of skin in the cat's voice box. When cats want to purr, they keep their vocal cords relaxed and just rattle the flaps together. Rather like the buzzing of a bumblebee's wings. If you can get your ear very close to a cat who's purring, you should be able to hear the sound stop every time the cat starts a new breath, which interrupts the buzzing for a fraction of a second.

Stretched out in the warm sun alongside her best friend, Libby feels really happy. There's only one thing bothering her, and that's the brightness of the sunlight. She loves its warmth, but being autumn, the sun is low in the sky, and the light hurts her eyes unless she keeps them shut tight. When you or I go out in bright sunlight, our pupils shrink down to the size of a pinhead, cutting down the amount of light that gets into our eyes.

Even then, we feel more comfortable wearing sunglasses, which aren't really practical for cats.

Cats' pupils are so big (allowing them to see at night) that they can't be shrunk down to a tiny circle. Instead, they close up into a slit with two tiny holes to let the light in, one at the top and the other at the bottom. Even then, sometimes cats find bright light uncomfortable. They will blink and half close their eyes, so that their eyelids cover both of the holes, leaving only the middle part of the slit for a bit of light to leak in.

Classes of Pupils

Dogs have round pupils like ours because, just like us, they mostly go out in the day and stay indoors at night.

Sheep and goats have a slit that goes from side to side so they can keep a look out all round. When they lower their heads to graze the grass, their eyes twist round so that the pupil stays horizontal.

Some lizards have slit pupils like cats do, but with several circular holes rather than just two.  Dolphins have crescent-shaped pupils which can be covered by a flap of skin when the light gets painfully bright, something that can happen just below the surface of the sea on a sunny day.

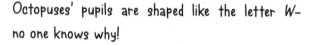

Octopuses' pupils are shaped like the letter W— no one knows why!

While Pippin dozes in the sun, Libby gently licks the back of his neck and around his ears. Cats love to have clean fur, and so they spend a lot of time grooming themselves with their raspy tongues. Your tongue is smooth on top, but a cat's is covered in tiny claw-shaped spines, perfect not only for cleaning fur, but also for rasping the last bits of meat off a bone. The problem with keeping your comb in your mouth is that it makes it hard to reach certain parts of your body.

Cats' tongues are quite long and flexible, but even they can't reach behind their ears! Cats who don't have cat friends deal with this by wiping their cheeks and the backs of their heads with the insides of their front legs, and then grooming those with their tongues as usual. But that's a pretty clumsy way of doing it, and cats who get on well will groom one another, just like Libby is doing to Pippin. Not just to keep each other clean and sweet-smelling, but also as a way of showing how much they like one another.

Watch This Space

After a while, Pippin wakes up and stretches. Then he jumps off the wall and heads back to his house. He doesn't say "goodbye" like you or I would, but Libby doesn't mind, because although cats have a way of saying "hello"—the upright tail— they don't seem to need to say anything when they part. Libby decides to go exploring for a while; some of these back gardens she knows well, others she doesn't. She heads straight for one of those gardens, along the top of a wall she's never walked on before.

All cats are very motivated to find out about the place where they are living. That's because in the days before cat food, their ancestors had to go out hunting every day just to get enough to eat. Dogs' lives revolve around their humans, but cats become very attached to the place where they live. When a family with a cat moves house, they seriously ought to keep the cat shut indoors for at least two weeks, especially if it's a completely new neighborhood. Cats don't understand that they may have been moved for hundreds of miles, because there's no way that their own legs could have carried them that far. They think that the place they used to live must be just around the corner.

If they do get out, they will keep looking for their old home until they get horribly lost. Which is actually what had happened to Libby when she arrived at Miss Lewis's house, although there's a twist to that story, as we shall see.

After two weeks in their new house, cats will have begun to feel comfortable there, and the memory of their old "patch" will have faded. The first time that a cat is let out in a new place, she will explore it very carefully.

She needs to learn two important things: how to find her way around without getting lost, and whether there are any dangerous animals around. So her first trip will most likely be a circuit of the back garden, keeping one eye on her escape route back into the house, in case something scary happens. Next time, she'll go a bit farther, maybe all around the house, so she can check out the front garden as well. The time after that, she may jump over a couple of walls, making sure that she remembers the way back. All the while, she will be building up a map of the neighborhood, not on paper or a screen like we would, but in her head.

After a few weeks, she will have gone as far as she feels comfortable, and her "map" will be complete. Her "map" won't just include houses and walls and garden sheds—it will also have the places where there are dogs, where other cats live, and where foxes go when they're out raiding garbage cans. And just like a map on paper, Libby can use hers to take shortcuts that she's never used before.

She's worked out that the wall she's walking on now will take her home more quickly than going the way she usually goes after meeting Pippin, and sure enough, she's soon back at the front of Miss Lewis's house.

There's a van parked on the driveway a couple of doors down, and seeing it makes Libby a bit worried, though she can't quite remember why. Very slowly she goes up to the front of the van and sniffs the front bumper. It's recently been rubbed on by a cat that Libby doesn't know, so she looks round quickly in case that cat is lurking somewhere nearby. In fact, the cat responsible is ten miles away in a different town, and has no idea that his scent-mark has traveled so far! The van belongs to the son of Miss Lewis's neighbor, and he comes round from time to time to help his mum fix things in the house.

Although she can't remember much about it now, it was in this van that Libby first arrived in this neighborhood. A long time ago, when she was just a young cat, she came across the van parked outside her old house with its rear doors open. She jumped inside for a closer look, and—*bang!*—the doors closed and she was stuck inside. No one heard her yowls for help, and she had to cling on tight to stop herself being thrown around as the van went round corners.

Finally the van stopped, the doors opened, and Libby was able to leap out through the legs of the most surprised driver!  She ran straight across the street and underneath a parked car. The van driver was not much of a cat person and soon gave up trying to coax her out. And that is the rest of the story of how Libby came to live with Miss Lewis.

Luckily for Libby, she doesn't really remember much about how scared she was for the few weeks after she had escaped from the van. Unlike humans, cats are mostly interested in what's going on right now. Libby doesn't ever think about the place where she used to live, or the people she used to live with. That's one of the big differences between cats and humans. Mae can still remember the orphanage very clearly and even feels a bit sad when she walks past their neighbors' house and catches the smell of North Indian cooking, reminding her of the place where she grew up. Luckily their neighbors sometimes invite Miss Lewis and Mae round for lunch!

Miss Lewis understands that cats become very attached to the place where they live, so it's usually best to leave them there when their owners go away on vacation. While she was in India to adopt Mae, another teacher in her school came in twice a day to feed Libby and check that she was OK. Catteries are fine, but most cats take a week or two to get used to them, so most are happier to stay at home for a short while even though their familiar humans are missing.

After her energetic morning, Libby's feeling a bit peckish (though not for spicy food), so she clatters back in through her cat flap. Her food bowl is empty, but there are still a few biscuits in her puzzle feeder, so she bats that around the floor for a while and eats all the biscuits that fall out.

Cats have small stomachs and like to eat several times each day, not just at our usual mealtimes. Way back when their ancestors were hunters, they would have to catch maybe ten mice a day, so eating little and often comes naturally to them. Dogs have much bigger stomachs and are happy with just one or two big meals a day.

It's warmer in the house than it is outside, so Libby settles down for a nap. Unlike you or me, most cats don't have a fixed routine.

They sleep when they feel like it, sometimes during the day and sometimes at night. Instead of being awake for fourteen or fifteen hours at a stretch, cats have several periods of activity spread out through the whole day and night. These often depend on what is going on around them, so, for example, Libby rarely dozes off during the evening when Miss Lewis and Mae are at home.

A quarter of an hour after she falls asleep, Libby's eyes begin to flutter beneath her closed eyelids, and from time to time her whiskers and tail twitch slightly. She must be dreaming, though only cats know what cats dream about. Their dreams last about ten minutes, and then repeat every fifteen minutes or so, if the cat stays asleep for that long.

Colors, Catnip, and Kiwi

Today, Libby wakes after an hour or so. She's feeling thirsty, but her water bowl is empty. For once, Miss Lewis has forgotten to top it off. It's important that cats get enough to drink, otherwise they can get an infection that makes peeing very painful. Luckily the kitchen tap is dripping (Miss Lewis hasn't gotten round to calling the plumber yet) so she jumps up onto the counter and lets a few drops fall into her mouth. Sometimes, when she's not so thirsty, Libby will bat the drips with her paw. Most cats find moving water fascinating—most likely just because it's moving—but hate getting wet, probably because their fur isn't waterproof like a dog's is, and so they get cold very quickly.

Now Libby's off outside again. This time, she heads in the opposite direction to this morning, squeezing through a tiny gap in a fence that's been damaged by a recent storm.

Before trying something like that, you or I would look carefully at a space to see if it was wide enough to get through, but cats don't need to bother. In any case, their eyes don't focus at short distances, so as Libby gets close to the gap, the edges go blurry. But that doesn't matter, because cats have whiskers! Cats know every time a whisker touches something, and they can tell just how wide a gap is by how much each whisker is bending backward. Thanks to her supple body, a gap that's big enough for her head is enough!

First her head, then her right shoulder, then her left shoulder, then the rest of her body, and Libby is through, saving herself a jump up and a jump down.

Libby reaches the children's playground at the end of the street. There are a few toddlers there, playing on the brightly colored swings and slides. Children love bright colors, but cats really aren't bothered about what color things are. That's because cats mainly see in black and white, even in the daytime. They can see a few colors, mostly greens and yellows, but while you might say "That slide is red," a cat would say "That's the slide that smells of fresh paint!" To cats, smells are more important than anything else. Libby is a bit nervous of children she doesn't know, so she keeps to the edge of the playground and slips through a gap in the hedge and into another garden.

This garden is special for Libby—and several other cats—because there are several old catnip plants at the back of an overgrown flowerbed, as well as a kiwi fruit vine growing on the side of a wall. Libby trots up to the catnip and sniffs—and a strange look comes into her eyes,

as if something has cast a spell on her.

She rubs her cheeks on it, then flops down on one side, rolling over and over on a branch of the catnip, purring away and appearing to have a wonderful time! This goes on for a few minutes, and then Libby seems to snap out of her trance; she shakes herself, quickly licks her sides where they've got dirty from all the rolling, and trots off again.

Not all cats like catnip (or catmint as it's sometimes called). In fact, about one cat in three can't smell catnip at all. No one knows why cats find catnip so fascinating, but it's not just domestic cats that love it. Lions, tigers, leopards, cougars, servals, and lynxes can all get excited about catnip.

Anyone who grows catnip in their garden has to get used to cats squashing the bushes.

The kiwi vine growing nearby is also showing signs of damage. Something has dug holes in the soil nearby, and the roots that have been exposed show signs of having been chewed—yes, it's cats again! Some cats think that kiwi roots smell a bit like catnip. There are some other plants that cause the same reaction, including the roots of an herb called valerian and one kind of honeysuckle. But not all cats respond to all of these plants—in fact, most only respond to a couple and some to none at all.

Whatever it is that these smells are doing to their brains, it doesn't seem to do them any harm. You can get toys for cats that contain one of these special plants, and these can provide a lot of fun for cats that can't go outdoors to find the plants themselves.

Cats DO Understand Us!

Now it's starting to get dark, reminding Libby that Mae and Miss Lewis will soon be home from school, so she heads back home. As she pushes through the cat flap, she hears Miss Lewis's key in the door and rushes to say hello. Up goes her tail, and she makes the little chirruping noise that mother cats make to keep in touch with their kittens. Not that Libby thinks that either Mae or Miss Lewis looks anything like a kitten, but cats don't have nearly as many ways of talking to people as dogs do, and chirruping is the best sound she can think of. Mae bends down and strokes her on the top of her head. "You've just come in, haven't you!" she says. "Your fur is chilly!"

People who don't like cats often say that cats don't like people, that they only hang around us because we feed them. But that's not true. Cats may not miss their owners much when they're left on their own, unlike dogs, who can get super upset. But they are very pleased to see their owners when they come back home. Of course, cats don't always like everyone they meet. They don't like people who are rough with them, or try to hug them too tightly; cats don't hug each other, except briefly when they're playing. Hugging is a human thing. But even though they don't always want to get too close, cats are very sensitive to how their owners are feeling. They watch us all the time and take note of the expressions on our faces and whether our voices sound cross or happy.

They know when we're talking to them, not so much because of what we're saying (which they don't understand much of) but because we're looking at them while we're speaking. And although a lot of people say they don't, pet cats *do* know the sound of their names, even when spoken by someone they don't know. But it's not fair to expect cats to come running up to you whenever they hear their names—that's a dog thing!

Cats have lived with people for thousands of years, so they probably understand more about us than we realize. When cats meet someone for the first time, somehow it only takes them a few seconds to decide whether that person likes cats. If they're worried that they might not, they'll mostly stay away from them. (Except that there are a few cats who always get it completely wrong, and jump up onto the laps of people who really don't want them there!)

When Mae came to live with Miss Lewis, Libby was the first friend she made. The moment she came in the front door, Libby was there with her tail up, and was rubbing round Mae's legs even before Miss Lewis had finished paying the taxi driver. Libby must have sensed straight away that Mae knew how to react to cats. Mae already knew that cats don't like being chased, even in a friendly way. Instead, they want people they don't know to stay still and wait until they are ready to approach that person. And cats are more likely to approach if people crouch down so they're not towering over the cat like some kind of giant.

Mae knew all about cats from her life in India. There had been lots of cats living around the orphanage, although they were all much skinnier than Libby! Lots of people fed them, but none of them had proper owners, and they used to wander in and out of the building all day, though they were usually shooed away in the evening. At first Mae thought it was rather odd that Libby was allowed to sleep in the house, but she soon got used to the idea, even when she and Libby became best friends and Libby took to sleeping at the end of her bed on cold nights.

Cats CAN Be Trained!

Miss Lewis is unpacking her bags full of schoolbooks, and while she waits for her dinner, Libby decides her claws need a good scratching. Miss Lewis is not especially materialistic, but she did start to get annoyed when Libby scratched the corner of the sofa and ripped the cloth. But she knew that there was no point in getting cross with Libby, who was doing something that's perfectly normal for cats to do, just in the wrong place. Instead, she went to the pet shop and bought two tall scratching posts, one covered in carpet, which she put in a corner of the upstairs landing, and another covered in rope. She had read that cats often don't use small scratching posts because they wobble about. She'd also read that different cats like different materials to dig their claws into: some prefer wood, some carpet, some rope, and others cardboard.

Miss Lewis put the rope-covered post right in front of the scratched corner of the sofa. She suspected that this was a place where Libby felt relaxed enough to scratch. When Libby started scratching the post instead of the sofa, Miss Lewis fed her a tasty treat as soon as she'd finished to show her that this was a good place to scratch. What she *didn't* do was drag Libby over to the post by her front legs and rub her paws down the post. She knew that would make Libby hate the post and never go near it again. Soon, Libby was using both scratching posts and she never damaged any of the furniture ever again.

The way Miss Lewis gave Libby treats for using the scratching post sounds like a sort of training—and that's exactly what it was. Everyone knows that dogs need training, but most people think that cats can't be trained. That's not true. Cats are very good at learning: who their friends are, where is safe to go and where isn't, when it's time for dinner, and so on. Training is just a way of helping a cat to learn to do the right things.

Dogs are easier to train than cats for two reasons. First, they are always paying attention to what their owners might be wanting them to do (although they can be distracted if there's something more exciting happening at the same time). Second, they love attention from their owners, and will do anything to get it. Some dogs will obey their owners just because they get praise when they've done the right thing. If you've ever seen a sniffer dog at an airport, he will have been trained using just a game and a snuggle.

There are a few cats who like being stroked so much that they can be trained the same way, and others who will do anything to get a game with their owner, but most cats respond best to a tasty morsel of food. Miss Lewis had looked this up, and so had some treats ready in the fridge (little pieces of roast chicken, Libby's favorite!).

Cats May Be Sweet, but Sweets Aren't for Cats!

Unlike dogs (and children!), cats really only like savory treats. Sweets mean nothing to them, because they can't taste sugar at all. In fact, no cats, from lions downward, can taste sweet things, and they aren't very good at digesting sugar, either. Animals that eat berries and other natural sweet treats need to know which ones are ripe and which are not and might give them a stomachache, so having a taste for sugar is useful. But cats of all sizes live on meat, so they don't need to check for sugars.

NO!   YES!

Instead, their tongues are super sensitive to the subtle differences between different meats, which is one reason why cats will sometimes refuse to eat food that smells perfectly OK to us.

Cats can also get stomachaches if they eat or drink too much sugar. Cow's milk contains a sugar called lactose which cats can't digest, so it's better to offer cats a milk that's specially made for them rather than ordinary milk straight from the bottle. And cats should always have fresh water to drink, especially if they eat a lot of dry biscuits.

NO!   YES!

When Miss Lewis brought a cat flap home from the pet shop, she decided to let Libby get used to it before she had it put into the door. She put the whole cat flap upright on the floor and held the actual flappy bit open. Libby had never used a cat flap before, and to begin with didn't have a clue what it was for. Some people think that a cat will learn how to use a cat flap if they push them through it, but actually that's more likely to make the cat scared of the flap. It's easier to train a cat to use a flap *before* it's put into the door.

First, Libby gave the flap a quick sniff, and then began to explore it with her nose and whiskers. The first time her face appeared in the opening, Miss Lewis dropped a piece of chicken on the floor close to the other side, so that Libby had to put her head through the hole to get it. Libby then thought she might get more treats by sitting on Miss Lewis's side of the flap and meowing, but Miss Lewis ignored her until she started exploring the flap again. The next time Libby looked through the hole, Miss Lewis dropped another treat. Through the gap went Libby's head, and now she was beginning to get what she was supposed to do. Each time she put her head through, Miss Lewis dropped the treat a bit farther away, persuading Libby to put her shoulders through, then her tummy, and finally her back legs as well.

Now that Libby had got used to going through the hole, she needed to learn to push the flap. First Miss Lewis held the flap half open while she repeated the training, so that Libby could get used to feeling the flap on the top of her head. Then, Miss Lewis gradually closed the flap further and further until Libby was pushing it on her own.

Now it was time to get the flap put into the back door. When the workman had gone, Miss Lewis let Libby sniff the flap a bit, so she could be sure it was still *her* flap (from the scent of her cheek and eyebrow glands from all that pushing). Then Miss Lewis picked up some treats and went into the garden, bent down by the flap and called Libby. Libby's face appeared behind the flap, then very cautiously she pushed it open—and Miss Lewis immediately popped a treat into her mouth! Soon Libby was using the cat flap like a pro, and training was over.

Who Invented the Cat Flap?

If you look on the internet, you'll probably read that Isaac Newton invented the cat flap. Isaac Newton was a very famous scientist who lived about three hundred years ago; he discovered gravity and invented the telescope, as well as lots of other important stuff. But probably not the cat flap. The story goes that when he was looking at the stars through his telescope and needed his room to be completely dark, his cat and her kittens used to push open the door to his workshop and let the light in, so he built them not just one but two special doors, one for the cat and the other for her kittens. But the kittens, seeing their mother using her flap, always followed her and never used theirs. However, other people say that Isaac Newton was too busy inventing things to have any time for any pets, neither cats nor dogs.

Cats Can Train Us, Too

Libby is really hungry now. Mae has gone upstairs to get changed, and Miss Lewis is taking longer than usual to sort out her schoolbooks, so Libby meows loudly to make sure her dinner hasn't been forgotten. Cats the world over meow to get people's attention, but they rarely meow to each other. Miss Lewis is fairly sure that Libby has at least three different meows. One means "Excuse me, but I'm hungry!" Another means "Please let me out!" and a third means "Bedtime!"

They do sound a bit similar, and Miss Lewis used to think that they could actually be the same meow, but done in different places—in the kitchen, by the back door (when Libby doesn't feel like using the cat flap) and at the foot of the stairs.

The funny thing about meows is that every cat does them differently. A few weeks before, Miss Lewis had taken part in a scientific experiment to find out what meows mean. She had to make a few recordings of each one of Libby's meows, and email them to the scientist. A few weeks later she got an email with eight meow recordings attached. Four were Libby's—she quickly spotted those— and four had been recorded from another cat. Miss Lewis could tell that those didn't sound the same, but when she was asked to say which meows were for food and which were asking to be let out, she only got one right (and that was just luck). Owners can tell what their own cat's meows mean, but other cats' meows are just meows.

No one is quite sure why this is, but here's a likely explanation. When cats are together, they keep an eye on one another, all the time. Humans are always looking at something else: phones, tablets, the TV, newspapers, books. Cats are smart, and quickly learn that the best way to get a human's attention is to make a noise—a meow.

Some never get any further than this; it's enough that they've trained their human to pay attention to them. Others develop lots of different meows for different situations. Mae thinks Libby has two meows, Miss Lewis thinks she has three. In fact, Libby can make five sorts of meows, but doesn't realize that Miss Lewis can't tell them all apart. It doesn't really matter, if they all get results!

How to Stroke a Cat

Libby finishes her dinner, and after a quick trip to the litter box, settles down on the sofa next to Miss Lewis, who is planning her schoolwork for tomorrow. Every now and again she reaches out to stroke Libby's head. Libby likes being touched on the head, but not really anywhere else. There are a few cats who like being stroked all over, but most have no-go areas. Most don't like to be touched on their tails, or on their backs just in front of their tails. And they hate it when little children, who don't know any better, grab their tail as they walk by.

A lot of cats don't like to have their bellies rubbed, either. Unfortunately, many cats roll on to their backs to show they like someone, but they are not necessarily asking for a tummy-tickle, however tempting that may be for the person. Some cats will accept a belly-rub for a few seconds but then find it all too much, and suddenly scratch the person's hand and jump away.

That's what happened to Mae the first time she tried to tickle Libby's belly, so she didn't try that again. It's best not to try tickling a cat's tummy, even when the cat seems to be inviting you to, unless you know the cat really well.

Similarly, some cats don't like being brushed, especially not in the places where they don't like to be stroked. Short-haired cats can usually keep their fur in tip-top condition, anyway, but long-haired cats can get knots and mats in their fur if they're not brushed regularly. If a cat needs brushing but doesn't like it, she can be trained to accept the brush by rewarding her with tasty treats. A soft brush is best, unless the cat's coat is really tangled. If you're not sure whether your cat is in the mood to be brushed, you can try stroking her on the head first to see if she then asks for more. Start at the head end where her tongue can't reach, and work backward. If the cat wanders off before you finish, let her. She'll probably finish the job herself, anyway!

When you are brushing, it's always best to stop if the cat starts getting restless, otherwise you could put them off the brush for life. The signs to watch out for are: twitching skin on the back, the tail thumping on the ground, the cat's body going tense, her ears going back, a sudden swallow or licking of the lips, or—obviously—a growl or a hiss. Stop *immediately*, and leave it for another day.

Playtime!

After dinner, Mae finishes her homework, and thinks about asking Miss Lewis if she can switch on the television. But she knows that would be boring for Libby. Most cats don't really understand television. The screens are a bit flickery for their sensitive eyes, and the bright colors are not very exciting for an animal that sees in black and white. If Libby hears a noise made by a cat, her ears may prick up, and once, the sound of kittens crying made her run round the back of the

TV to see if they were trapped there! Cats do like some kinds of music, though, especially if it's been written specifically for them, with lots of birds singing and purring noises as part of the tune. Then they may start purring themselves and even rub their cheeks on the speakers. But TV shows made for humans are not great for sharing with cats.

Miss Lewis has seen the weather forecast, and knows that it's likely to be raining for the next few days. That will keep Libby indoors more than usual, and Miss Lewis doesn't want her to get fed up while she's alone in the house. While Libby's having a stretch, Miss Lewis gets her box of toys out of a cupboard and gives it to Mae. It's playtime!

Cats love to play, especially when they're young. Kittens do play with one another, but it's not easy for a person to copy the way a kitten plays. What starts out as an innocent game of rough-and-tumble with a grown-up cat may be misunderstood and turn into an actual fight, resulting in scratched hands and a grumpy cat! Luckily, even grown cats really love hunting games.

Mae picks out a table tennis ball and rolls it across the floor. Libby runs after it, swiping at it over and over again with her paws so that it bounces from one corner of the room to another.

Cats will also chase the red dot of a laser pointer, but some experts think that is a kind of teasing, since when the cat does pounce on the light, there's nothing they can actually touch with their paws. So a ball is probably better.

After a while, Libby loses interest in the ball, so Mae puts it away in the box and gets out another toy. This is a small fishing rod with an imitation spider on the end of the line. Mae jerks the line in front of Libby's nose, and Libby swipes at it with her paws.

When Mae raises the rod, Libby rears up on her hind legs as if it were a bird she is chasing. This is fun! Then after a few minutes she gets a bit bored with the spider toy and sits down. But she's still watching Mae intently, because she knows that there are more games to play. Even though Libby's sitting down and looking relaxed, she grooms her shoulder very quickly a couple of times, which shows that she's still super alert.

The next toy is a little furry mousey thing. Mae throws it across the room and Libby chases and pounces. She grasps the toy between her front paws and bites into it, then lets go with her paws and shakes her head so that the toy flies into the air. Off she goes again, chasing and pouncing until that toy, too, seems to have become a bit boring.

The final toy is a big furry animal, almost as big as Libby herself. Again, Mae throws it and again Libby chases and pounces, but this time she doesn't bite. Instead, she flops onto her side, holding the toy in her front paws, and kicks it with her back paws, until she loses her grip and the toy slides away. Libby turns and looks at it, but seems unsure whether she wants to pounce again. So Mae gets the fishing rod toy out again, and Libby happily plays with that for a while.

Mae is enjoying the game almost as much as Libby is, but Libby hardly looks up at her while she's concentrating on the toy spider. She doesn't even seem to realize that it's Mae who's making the spider move. Cats are not good at noticing when things are connected together. Many kinds of animals can be trained to get food by pulling it toward them on a string—but not cats!

If you watch a cat playing with toys, you'll see that everything they do looks like they are chasing a mouse or something like that. Cats can't forget that they once had to hunt for a living. That's why cats play for longer when they're hungry. Birds were there to be grabbed out of the air, mice to be pounced on. A rat would make a feast, but might fight back and cause a nasty wound. That's the reason why Libby wasn't quite so keen on the big furry toy, and played with it at paw's length. Nowadays most of us don't like our cats to kill little animals, but experts have discovered that encouraging them to hunt toys makes them less interested in hunting for real.

Libby did bring a dead bird into the house, just the once. Truth is, she hadn't killed it herself—its neck had broken when it flew into next door's patio window. (Fact: In some cities, more birds are killed flying into windows than are killed by cats.) A cat's instinct is to take anything that it might want to eat to a safe place, like indoors. But Miss Lewis thought Libby had killed it, and couldn't help shouting at her. Libby never did it again! But she wasn't upset. It's a myth that cats bring their kills indoors as "presents" for their owners. They are just taking their prey somewhere safe before they eat it—and once they get inside they probably remember that their cat food is tastier than bird or mouse, and so abandon it!

Are You Left-Handed or Right-Handed?

When Libby swipes at a toy, she always uses her left paw first. Miss Lewis is left-handed, and wonders whether Libby might have copied her. But Libby has been left-pawed since she was a young cat, long before she met Miss Lewis. Unlike humans, who are mostly right-handed, there are as many left-pawed cats as there are right-pawed. Other cats don't have a favorite paw, and for some reason these cats are often less friendly than cats who do have a favorite. Beware the ambidextrous cat!

Cats love hunting games, but they also love exploring. Sometimes when Miss Lewis goes out to work she leaves a couple of old cardboard boxes on the floor for Libby to investigate. If she has time, she will cut some holes in the sides of one of the boxes, just big enough for Libby to squeeze through. When she comes home, she often finds Libby has

crammed herself into one of the boxes and is fast asleep. Which makes Mae and Miss Lewis laugh! Libby would rather be outdoors, but if it's raining, a cardboard box will keep her amused.

Some cats have to be kept indoors all the time. For example, cats that live in flats, cats whose owners live near busy roads, cats who live in neighborhoods where other cats attack them as soon as they go out. It's possible to teach a cat how to walk on a lead like a dog, so that's one way of giving them exercise and new experiences (not to mention all the attention the person walking the cat will get!). Indoor cats can also be kept amused by giving them their own spaces to explore: cat-sized tunnels, or places to rest high up where they can see what's going on without having to join in. You can buy these ready-made from a pet shop, but they're easy to make out of cardboard boxes and some tape—and these are quick and cheap to replace if the cat gets bored (or tears them to pieces!).

Time for Bed

Miss Lewis puts the toys away, and Mae goes upstairs to get ready for bed. Libby settles down on the sofa again while Miss Lewis listens to the radio. Soon it gets late, and Miss Lewis goes around the house, turning out the lights. When she goes to lock the back door, Libby meows, puts her tail up, rubs against her leg, and looks up at her. "Do you really want to go out?" asks

Miss Lewis. She opens the door. It's already raining. Libby sits on the mat for a moment, then turns back into the house, purring and winding herself around Miss Lewis's legs. Miss Lewis is rather tired and finds this slightly irritating, but Libby is only being friendly.

Some people say that cats are sly, cold, mischievous creatures with no feelings. But Libby's purring and rubbing shows that she is very fond of Miss Lewis. She rubs and purrs when she's with her cat-friend Pippin, but not nearly so much as she does when she's with Miss Lewis (or Mae).

Now it's Miss Lewis's bedtime. Up the stairs she goes, followed ten minutes later by her faithful feline. Libby settles down on Miss Lewis's feet and purrs them both to sleep. But only for a couple of hours, when Libby has a prowl around the house, before heading upstairs again to sleep, this time in Mae's bedroom. Cats like to have a few sleeping places to choose from, depending on how cold or warm it is, or even just so they can have a change every now and again. Then just before dawn Libby wakes. She grooms herself for a couple of minutes before heading downstairs, *click-clack* and out through the cat flap for her morning patrol. Go carefully, Libby!

ACKNOWLEDGMENTS

A big thank-you to all the humans who helped me with this book, especially Beatrice and Sam Bradshaw; Melanie Pressey; Bella, Sylvie, and Alice Penfold; Senan and Marcy Bestic; Clare Elsom for bringing Libby to life; Dr. Sarah Brown; Professor David Hopkins; John Ash; Patrick Walsh; Chloe Sackur; and Eloise Wilson.

Author Questions & Answers

Hello, John!

What made you decide to become an anthrozoologist?

I'm a biologist, and most biologists study wild animals. But I realized that the pet animals who live in our houses are just as fascinating, so I decided to study them instead.

What's the most exciting thing you discovered when studying cats?

Many people think that cats are selfish creatures that don't need friends to be happy, but that isn't true at all. Cats often aren't as over-the-top affectionate as dogs are, but they have their own ways of showing that they are fond of their owners—for example, when they stick their tails up in the air and rub round our legs. That's exactly the same way that kittens say hello to their mothers, and who could deny that kittens love their mums? Cats can be very sociable animals; pet cats simply have different priorities to pet dogs. For dogs, people always come first. Cats need to have a safe place to live in before they can relax and show their loving side.

If you could have a cat's hearing, eyesight, or smell, which would you choose and why?

I'd like to have a cat's sense of smell. A cat's eyesight isn't much better than our own, except at dawn and dusk, and I would miss being able to see the bright colors that our eyes give us, but cats' eyes don't.

The same goes for hearing: Cats can hear what bats are saying to each other, but I'd rather keep my ability to hear the tiny variations in pitch and texture that make music so enjoyable. The sense of smell has intrigued me ever since I started studying animals, and although cats can't smell everything that dogs can, their noses still pick up a lot that ours miss entirely. Wouldn't it be fascinating if we could find out what's been going on in the garden overnight just by having a sniff around early in the morning? But would the change make me like the smell of cat food? Surely not!

If you could be any animal, what would you be? And why?

Well, apart from being a cat, I'd fancy being a bird or a fish, so I could find out what it's like to fly or to live underwater.

If you had a superpower that allowed you to talk to cats, what would you ask your pet cat?

I'd love to know what cats are trying to tell us when they move their tails about. From our studies, we know that an upright tail means "I'm feeling friendly," but cats' tails seem so expressive that I'm sure they must be trying to use them to talk to us in all sorts of ways. Why do cats sometimes curl the tip of their tail, making a shape a bit like a question mark? What does it mean when cats wag their tails from side to side? Does a sudden twitch of the tail mean something different to a slow swish? I'm sure that if people understood more about what their cat was trying to tell them, they'd enjoy their company so much more.